But one thing is necessary

Luke 10:42

Diaconal Silence

A Guide for Making a Retreat

Deacon James Keating, Ph.D.

En Route Books and Media, LLC
Saint Louis, MO

En Route Books and Media, LLC
5705 Rhodes Avenue
St. Louis, MO 63109

Contact us at
contactus@enroutebooksandmedia.com

Cover Credit: Sebastian Mahfood

Copyright 2025 Institute for Diaconate Renewal

ISBN-13: 979-8-88870-484-4
Library of Congress Control Number: 2025951444

All rights reserved. No part of this book may be reproduced, stored in a retrieval system, or transmitted in any form, or by any means, electronic, mechanical, photocopying, or otherwise, without the prior written permission of the author.

Imprimatur

In accordance with CIC 827, permission to publish has been granted on February 10, 2026 by Very Reverend Father Carl Scheble, Vicar General, Archdiocese of St. Louis. Permission to publish is an indication that nothing contrary to Church teaching is contained in this particular work. It does not imply any endorsement of the opinions expressed in the publication, or a general endorsement of any author; nor is any liability assumed by this permission.

Quotes

"There is need of only one thing. Mary has chosen the better part, and it will not be taken from her."

— *Luke 10:42*

"For thus said the Lord God, the Holy One of Israel: In returning and rest you shall be saved; in quietness and in trust shall be your strength."

— *Isaiah 30:15*

"Come away by yourselves to a deserted place and rest awhile."

— *Mk 6:31*

"Abide in me, as I abide in you. Just as a branch cannot bear fruit on its own unless it remains on the vine, so neither can you unless you remain in me."

— *John 5:14*

The Spirit's "word is heard by all in the most attentive silence; through the impetus of love, the unmoved yet most perfect mover infuses itself into all."

— *St. Mary Magdalene de Pazzi*

Table of Contents

Quotes i

Foreword v

Introduction: Why Silence? 1

How to Pray 13

Practical Matters: From Activity to Silence 19

Lectio Divina 23

Practical Matters: *Lectio Divina* 29
    Where To Pray 31
    How to Pray This Way 31

Adoration 35
    How do we adore, and what is the relationship between Adoration and Lectio Divina? 38

Practical Matters: *Adoration* 45

What is Spiritual Direction on a Retreat? 49

What is Spiritual Consolation / Desolation? 57

Meditation Questions 61

Interior Silence 65

Conclusions 69

Endorsements.. 71

About the Author 75

Foreword

What is a silent-directed retreat? It is a classic path where intimacy with Trinitarian love can be experienced away from our duties and responsibilities. Through intimacy with God's love, silence becomes preferred. This silence carries God's love into our hearts and protects it there.

Being in love with God engenders a sense of well-being. This inspires us to crave more of God's love.

Such an exchange of love also inspires action that is pleasing to God and fruitful for others. Knowing that God loves us matures us emotionally. Such affective maturity is rooted in desires satisfied…desire for intimacy with God. Accompanying this silent prayer is growth in the Spirit, manifested by an increase in the virtues and fruits of the Spirit: "love, joy, peace, patience, kindness, generosity, faithfulness, gentleness, self-control" (Gal. 5:22-23). This is what the Directory calls integral human development (see *The National Directory for the Formation, Ministry, and Life of Permanent Deacons in the United States of America* 2nd Edition, 113; 117; 122; 135; 225, etc.)

The Institute for Diaconate Renewal is dedicated to offering silent retreats as a path of ongoing conversion, human growth in affective maturity, and spiritual renewal for deacon formators, their formation associates, deacons, their wives, and deacon spiritual directors.

Don't just read this book. It is written to stimulate reflection on our relationship with God. Pray through this book while on retreat or after it.

This booklet is written as a practical help for deacons and others making a silent-directed retreat. The publication of this booklet is made possible through the generosity of the J. Allan Mitchell Foundation. We are grateful for their support and encouragement.

The Co-Directors of IDR, Deacons Mark Erste, MA, and Stephen F. Miletic, PhD, wish to express their appreciation to deacons Stephen Miller, MA, Christopher Ast, and Scott Dodge, D.Min., alongside Dr. Christopher Burgwald, STD, for their generosity in reading this work pre-publication.

Introduction

Why Silence?

It is rare for a deacon to enter into silence as the mode of his annual retreat. Most deacons attend retreats that are not real retreats but conferences, workshops, or seminars. These gatherings are filled with talking and peppered with prayer. These "retreats" function as occasions for diaconal fellowship and ongoing formation, but they resist the intimidating path that effectively leads one into God's presence: silence. Our silent encounters with God's Presence and Love are both the beginning and goal of contemplative prayer.

This resistance to silence is based upon the cultural content of diaconal formation. The content is usually academic; it is functional, pragmatic, and efficient. It is the opposite of contemplative. In fact, I was told by several deacon directors that "deacons are not naturally contemplative; they are doers and possess little interest in the interior life." If this is true, it may be due to how diaconal formation programs have been structured in the United States. Diaconal formation is ordered toward pastoral competency and doctrinal familiarity. Of course, there are programs that aim for more than doctrinal "familiarity" since they require deacons to gain a master's degree in theology or some related field. What most programs miss, due to their structure, is the intentional cultivation of interior prayer. And so, when "retreats" are offered by dioceses, they mirror and extend how deacons were initially formed. Thus, the "retreats" further one's competency in pastoral ministry or doctrinal knowledge. They also function as a means of fellowship with other deacons of the diocese. What they don't emphasize is deepening interior silence, intimacy in contemplative prayer, and sustained spiritual direction. Normally these qualities were never integrated into a deacon's initial formation. The aim of formation was practical not contemplative. But how can men proclaim and preach if such homilies do not originate from an interior silence **necessary** for personal communion with the Holy Trinity? Homilies are not classes; homilies are prayer-like, spoken aloud so the preacher can draw the congregation into prayer. The Eucharistic Liturgy is a prayer. It is the action of Christ's offering the Father true worship. If deacons only possess discursive knowledge about Christ but have an undeveloped intimacy with Christ, how will their homilies serve the end and purpose of the Mass?

If deacons are not "naturally contemplative," can

they become so through formation? Is it necessary that they become contemplatives? I would have to say that it is necessary if we consider deacons to be spiritual and liturgical leaders. Are they? Or are they simply attendants and helpers and practitioners? If this is the common understanding of diaconal identity, then most retreats simply confirm this diminished view of diaconal life: it is functional. Certainly, diaconal fellowship, ongoing formation, and doctrinal updating are all goods to be pursued. Indeed, they are. But if the diaconate is an intrinsically spiritual vocation, one ordered toward leading others into the mysteries of Christ's own gift of self, the deacon should be the first recipient of such intimate love and life. Some dioceses are beginning to understand this. They are starting to offer silent retreats as an annual option alongside the more traditional "retreat-workshop" weekend. I would hope that someday the silent retreat becomes the new norm and that workshop/fellowship gatherings simply offer the goods they were meant to offer. And these goods do not "count" as a retreat.

Why would a silent retreat be better for deacons? Two reasons: 1) deacons are a grade of Holy Orders;

2) deacons carry within them the potential for celibacy. Both reasons point to the nature of the diaconate being supernatural. The deacon is about God. He is not a social worker, a societal "do-gooder," a pastoral helper, or an ecclesial manager.

First, a deacon is to be fascinated by God. Why else would a married deacon promise to be celibate if his wife predeceases him? The only good reason to enter the diaconate — knowing that one day you may live without a wife — is because you are already sure that God is fascinating enough to support you in a life of celibacy. Celibacy is not merely an ecclesial requirement because clerics are so busy that it is unjust to be married. Celibacy is not just a convenience for a bishop in the matter of his assigning his priests and deacons with more ease. Now, of course, there are some priests and deacons who place celibacy in the category of convenience or pragmatism. But what kind of man would give up the companionship and beauty of a woman for efficiency? There is only one normal, rational reason to forego the companionship and beauty of woman…this man has met the Source of the woman's beauty. He has had an encounter with that Source and knows the Source to be a real living union of Three Divine Persons. The Three Persons are so real that one can commune with Them for an entire lifetime or part of an entire lifetime as a celibate. These Eternal Persons are so real that their divine beauty presents itself as a vocation, as an invitation from God for God to become one's first interest.

When such a man meets Beauty itself, God, he becomes a contemplative. He becomes someone who wants to marvel in love over the life, death, and resurrection of Christ. He becomes one desirous of prayer. Such a man is what most Catholics think clergy are: Men who know and are known by the Most Holy Trinity. This is why they seek deacons out for shared prayer or a blessing. This is why they listen to deacons preach or teach. They think deacons know God. Deacons are not men who have simply undergone ecclesial training to "help out" around the diocese. Deacons are men fascinated with God. Being formed by and in such fascination is the content of authentic diaconal formation. And it is only because of this fascination that a man is then formed in pastoral ministry or becomes competent in teaching doctrine. Fascination with God is the foundation for all deacon formation and fellowship. Fascination with

God is what authentic diaconal formation should confirm and deepen over years. Fascination with God invites prayer.

In prayer, a man realizes that he wants the Holy Spirit to configure him to Christ and His own Servant Mysteries. These Servant Mysteries are actions that Christ Himself did during His time on earth *(see Lk 10:29ff; 14:15-23; 17:7- 10; 22:27; Jn.13:14-15).* He now wants these actions to continue in the soul and body of a deacon. The first and most vital mystery a deacon hosts in his own body is the action of Christ heralding the Good News, and the second most vital mystery flows from having this Living Word of God dwell within his body and soul: enacting the charity of Christ. The deacon is a man configured to the preaching and compassionate heart of Christ. The reason one might seek out a retreat ordered by only silence is so that what happened at ordination objectively continues to be secured subjectively over time in and through prayer. Ongoing formation and fellowship aid this securing, but only prayer effects that a man will not become adrift from the mysteries that wounded him with their beauty on ordination day.

Deepening contemplative prayer, intimacy

with the mysteries of Christ, is required by the very nature of the diaconate itself. The most effective agent for deepening such contemplative intimacy is silence. Such intimacy with God might at first be a motivation to keep deacon retreats in the category of workshop or ongoing formation. Intimacy can induce fear. We become intimate with God in the same way one does with a wife: we share our hearts and receive in return her revealed heart. In this mutual self-revelation, one internalizes the beloved. Without intimacy, without risking vulnerable self-revelation, communion cannot be attained. Without intimacy, one remains an acquaintance, a collaborator, and colleague. Only intimacy attains what Christ calls us into with himself: friendship.

At ordination one has certainly entered a vulnerable relationship with God. The one to be ordained prostrates upon the sanctuary floor. This act of bodily surrender is to be forever lived out as the surrender of the heart to the Sacred Heart of Christ. The surrendered heart orders and defines the intimacy begun on ordination day. The exchange of hearts, the revelation of and reciprocity between one's inner life with the heart of God is the nature of contemplative prayer. Since Christ wants us to enter eternal life by sacramentally hosting His body in ours, our calling is to contemplate such generous love. We are called to gaze in love with our inner eye upon the beauty of Christ's own Servant Mysteries. We access these mysteries in a prayerful reading of Scripture and as we immerse ourselves within the Eucharistic Liturgy itself.

Deacons must be contemplatives, or they cannot understand their supernatural vocation. A retreat is gifted to us so that we may stay faithful to our true vocation as contemplatives even in action. We are invited to discern all our ministerial actions in the light of our communion with the Holy Trinity. Deacons do not initiate ministry; they are sent on mission. And one cannot be sent until one listens to God in prayer. Very often, deacons "take" a ministry. They notice in all good will the many needs of a diocese and set out to "help" or "solve problems." This kind of attitude may work in business or the military or social work, but men taken up into a supernatural vocation are invited to pray and be sent. There is a role for creativity in ministry, for noticing human need, but our response to such must be born of contemplative obedience. If the ministry is to bear fruit it must originate in God's goodness, a goodness we discern through contemplative prayer wrapped in silence.

You have entered retreat to deepen your capacity for listening to God, contemplating His Servant Mysteries, and embracing your emissary status as a cleric sent from the altar into the heart of human need. Your capacity to listen, to contemplate, and to obey will all mature with each yearly silent-directed retreat you make. Silence will soon become what you desire most on any retreat, and a companion to listen to your stilled heart in spiritual direction will become a trusted source for growth in intimacy with God. Retreats are meant to secure, deepen, and stabilize your intimacy with God. Fellowship, education, and pastoral updating can all be accomplished in other proper and effective venues.

The retreat is for that exclusive and sacred time of communicating with God from within the specific vocation we have as men in Holy Orders. Let's take a closer look at the components of a silent-directed retreat so that we can enter this time anticipating positive consequences within our prayer life.

How to Pray

As we enter retreat, we need time to transition from the activity of our secular and ministerial commitments into an environment which facilitates intimacy with God. Retreat is simply the choice to enter the desert. In a silent-directed retreat, we move ourselves from an environment of activity and distraction and enter one where we can receive and be received by God. To some extent, entering a retreat means experiencing a vacuum wanting to be filled with all the commitments and duties we left "behind" in our everyday life. As we settle into the retreat house, we may find that our minds keep cycling through what work and duties await us when we return or those which remain unfinished as we left to journey to the retreat house. Give yourself some time to simply find your room and sit in the chair provided there. As you are sitting, notice each worry or forgotten duty that passes through your mind and simply release it into Christ's heart. He will guard these realities for you. If you need to, write these sources of anxiety or concern down on paper and resolve to attend to them when the retreat has finished. Ask the Holy Spirit now to simply give you the grace of remaining in His presence for the remainder of the retreat. What we are doing as the retreat begins is genuinely like the transition we make from work to a date night. We prepare for the date after the work day is complete, transition into a new place, renounce any reality that might intrude to derail our goal of simply attending to one's date and her presence (e.g., turn off phone, do not talk about work, etc.), and then we remain in her presence through communication. A retreat is similar, except our date is God.

Communication is the key to a successful date, and it is the same with making a fruitful retreat. Communication on retreat is called prayer. Communication is the means for two persons to reveal their hearts to one another and over time through this communication become mutually internalized in one another's heart. This mutual internalization is called intimacy, and it is the very reason those who love wish to remain in communication. Intimacy is the antidote to loneliness and emotional isolation. God said that to live in emotional isolation is "not good for man" (Gen. 2:18). Hence, we go on dates and retreats. As the retreat begins how are we to enter communication with God?

The retreat will suggest various simple ways, but of

course there are many ways to achieve and remain in intimacy with God. All such ways have one fundamental character: surrendering the heart and mind to God in silence. As one example, the silent-directed retreat led by the *Institute for Diaconate Renewal* begins the great surrender to God by allowing an Icon to direct the retreatants eyes, mind, and heart to note any interior responses. The retreatants also note any interior resistance to the Icon's promptings. This kind of experience is contemplative prayer in action. Praying before an icon is sometimes called *visio divina; sacred beholding.* We gaze in love upon the mystery of God in paint, in image.

Also, we are invited to enter communication with God through the prayerful reading of Scriptures. This is called Sacred Reading or *lectio divina* in Latin. We are invited into Eucharistic Adoration, at which we lovingly and silently adore God in wonder over the Incarnation of His Son. Further, we are invited to worship Him at Mass. And finally, we are invited to communicate with Him in spiritual direction. Beyond these simple ways, remember that the whole environment of silence enveloping you is also a way to go into the presence of God. Through silence, we can remain with God throughout the day. Again, be patient with yourself as you transition into silence. The "*noise*" that inhabits our minds and hearts is reticent to leave simply by our entering silence. This "noise" may take a while to realize it was not invited on the retreat. We will reflect more on silence and spiritual direction as we go along, but for now, we will concentrate upon *lectio* and the Eucharist.

Practical Matters

From Activity to Silence

"But one thing is necessary … "

— Luke 10:42

- Act of Trust & Faith — At the beginning, surrender your whole self to Christ. Ask for the grace of deeper intimacy with the Trinity.

- Breathing — close your eyes, breathe slowly in through the nose, out through the mouth. After about 5-10 minutes, your lungs will transmit more oxygen to your blood, and that blood will feed your brain.

- "Noise" — emerges when we begin to calm down. "What shows up inside" are a flood of images, rational thinking and emotional experiences. Let go of the "*noise*" *(the important, the urgent, the necessary)*.

- Continue to breathe and surrender these all to God.

- One of the fruits of struggling with and surrendering "noise" to God during the retreat will be the interior "decompression" or "detoxing." It could take a couple of days; receive it as it begins to "arrive"!

Lectio Divina

On a date, the woman expects us to talk to her. It is the greatest expectation of any date. This is why dates usually are constructed to encourage conversation. The couple will go for a walk or a quiet dinner. If they attend an event, they will naturally choose to be together in a quiet place for coffee or a drink upon its conclusion. They have come together FOR communication. And so, communication will win out if the couple is to remain together.

On retreat, God wants to communicate with you and you with Him. We have found, however, that God has communicated a great deal already in the Life, Death, and Resurrection of His Son, and in the Covenants of the Old Testament. All this communication is called the Bible. And so, we naturally go to the Bible first to do what anyone who wishes to attain intimacy with another does: listen.

Praying with Scripture can occur in the silence of your room at the retreat house, in the chapel, or in a comfortable seat outdoors. The first thing we ought to do before opening the Scripture is to ask the Holy Spirit to come to us and remain with us as we prayerfully read and listen to the content of the Bible. But where should we start this prayerful reading? The Scripture is certainly large. Should we start with

Genesis? On retreat, like a first date, one may start the conversation following the interests or desires of your heart. There is no fixed rule. I usually suggest that one start with a Gospel, or with the prayer that Christ himself prayed: the Psalms. But again, just open to where you feel attracted and expect that God's revelation of His mind and heart will be encountered (Eph. 1:17; 4:23; Col 3:10).

What should we be doing as God is speaking? In *lectio divina* the goal is to listen until we hear something. When we hear something, that is when what we are reading in God's revelation affects us personally, we should stop reading and simply let that portion of what God is saying work its way into our hearts. For example, if you are praying with the death of Christ upon the cross and come upon His words "Father, into your hands I commend my spirit" (Lk. 23:46) and they pierce your heart, move your affect, or light up your intellect, you should pause and begin to welcome this movement at a deeper level of your prayer. Meet such movements with "Lord what more do you want to say to me about this passage?" or "Why Lord did these words cause such a reaction in my heart?" Allow the Lord to answer you or simply take you deeper into His presence. Always remember that God may not immediately communicate an answer to our questions during our prayer. He often answers prayers later in the day as we are moving through our daily schedule. Be hospitable to such "visits" from God. Keep your heart open all day long. Such is the disposition of recollection. In this disposition, one is quiet within, guarding the door of the heart from superficial ideas or passing emotions, and remaining alert to deeper movements of God's Spirit within the heart. These movements may carry an answer or further communication by God, which had begun earlier in your *lectio divina* time.

What is *affect*? Affect is our emotional life, which is deeper than just passing moods or emotions. Affect is connected to the intellect (including the imagination) and will. It includes our desires, thoughts, imagination, and feelings.

Said another way, affective movements are not passing emotional moods but deeper movements within the soul bringing us closer to or separating us from God. When we receive consolation or desolation, for example, these are experienced as deeper emotional movements not created by ourselves. It is the Lord working within our hearts. Knowledge of our interior life is grounded in knowledge of what kind of affective movements are working in our hearts. Being attentive to our affective movements helps us to grow in our awareness of God working within our souls.

How should we respond to God's word? The purpose of communicating with God is to allow Him to find us. He wants to call us out of hiding in sin (Gen. 2:8; Ps. 139:23-24; Eph. 5:11-13) so we might live in His presence. Objectively, we were saved from eternal damnation at baptism, but subjectively our "work" is to stay in love with God through the spiritual and moral life. Our prayer life has one goal, to keep us in communion with God. Staying in communion with God and away from the isolation of sin is our most noble calling. We respond to God's Word by remaining in Him (Jn. 15:4), by communicating with Him, by acting out of this communion, and by rejecting self-sufficiency.

Practical Matters

Lectio Divina

"But one thing is necessary … "

— Luke 10:42

Where To Pray

- Find the place where you feel comfortable praying. Again, it can be in the chapel, your room, or on the retreat house grounds.
- The location may change over the length of the retreat.

How to Pray This Way

- Ask the Holy Spirit to come and guide your prayerful reading.
- Identify and acknowledge how you are feeling right at this very moment. This is the first step in listening. Eventually or immediately, we transition from listening to ourselves to hearing God speak to our hearts. The grace here can be moving from a conversation with my real self to a conversation with the real Holy Spirit.
- Ask the Lord which part of Scripture He wants you to spend time in. Your attraction

to a particular book can be understood as His answer. Or the retreat outline could have recommended Scriptures for each of the morning and afternoon sessions. You may start there; and if drawn to something else, go there.

- Follow the fundamental rule: respond to the Holy Spirit leading you.
- Begin to read, and as you read be aware of when you detect an attraction to a certain word, sentence, or image. These attractions can be the beginning of affective movements.
- Pause from your reading and begin to converse with the Spirit. Is that you Lord? What do you wish to say or give to me?
- Rest in this communion *(or the affective movement which has caught your imagination)* for a while, until the insight or affect filled with His Presence dissipates naturally.
- If no discernible insight or sense of divine presence is given or deepened at the place you paused, then continue to read or go to the next passage. Follow this same pattern for the length of time of your reading.

Practical Matters: *Lectio Divina* 33

- You should give about 15 to 30 minutes for *lectio divina.*
- Afterwards, you may want to write down in a journal any graces you received or questions that arose during this prayer time. Discuss these with your spiritual director.

It is vital that a deacon immerse himself in the Word this way as he is the proclaimer of the Gospel at Mass. *Lectio divina*, therefore, is not simply a mode of prayer but an essential devotion through which a deacon internalizes what was entrusted to him on his ordination day: the Book of the Gospels.

# Adoration

The whole of the Gospels is present in the Eucharist. When a deacon comes to adore the Lord in the Blessed Sacrament, he is entering the presence of God's actions enfleshed. His main action was to come among us and reveal God to us. Upon this revelation, many are compelled to remain in God's presence: "Master, where do you live?" (Jn. 1:38) When humans are vulnerable to the Incarnation, when they risk being affected by it, very often they want to remain with Him. But this remaining in prayer is twofold. We remain with Christ because he is God, Triune, and Love itself, and as St. Augustine said, "no one eats the flesh of Christ without first adoring it." Our prayer before the Eucharist intensifies and further internalizes, through contemplation, what we participated in at daily Mass. We receive Christ more intentionally, more profoundly, as we live a life of participation in the Mass and the commitment to prolong that participation through contemplation of the Eucharist in adoration.

Further, for the deacon it is essential to know that the Church teaches this personal encounter with the Lord, this Eucharistic Adoration, is what strengthens our ministry (see Benedict XVI, *Sacramentum Caritatis* 2007, no. 66f). Since we receive and adore the

Christ who is Charity, who is God reaching those in pain, reaching those who lack, and reaching those in need both materially and spiritually, our allowing this personal divine presence to reach us in Eucharistic contemplation can only renew our diaconal ministry.

Such ministry is Christ's, so He wishes to strengthen us, inspire us, and sustain us in it through contemplation of the Eucharist, His very Sacred Heart.

How do we adore, and what is the relationship between Adoration and *Lectio Divina*?

During a retreat, we immerse ourselves in silence to fast from the "noise" that is Western popular culture. It will take some hours before external silence can chase away the usual "noise" that runs through our hearts. Being with Christ in a posture of Adoration hastens our being possessed by silence.

From the interior silence with which the Holy Spirit gifts us, we notice affective movements filled with divine communication. God is reaching us from within. In Adoration we surrender to the Real Presence of Christ. This surrender is our will making itself available to Him. In Adoration, we want to be affected by God. We surrender to Him so that we make ourselves hospitable to His love. The result of all Adoration is a deeper faith, hope, and love. Adoration may move our feelings, but such movement is not the prime purpose of this prayer. The purpose is to worship and adore God. In doing so, we will become more adept at receiving divine love. Adoration, if done regularly, beyond any retreat, internalizes our communion with God. We want to be men who can immediately move into communion with God at any point of the day, in any circumstance. We want to be characterized as men who turn their will toward God with ease, who delight in having God closer to us than we are to ourselves. Ask the Holy Spirit for this grace of knowing God personally, experientially (Eph. 1:17).

A deacon matures in this Adoration which secures an interior life. It is this interior life, one of communion with the Holy Trinity, that becomes the fertile source of all his homilies, counsel, and teaching. Such ministry has its origin in and flows from such holy communion. The deacon who adores is a man who knows God. Because of this knowledge, people will be blessed by his ministry. They will not be with a man who mastered data; they will be with a man who possesses wisdom born of suffering the love of God and the death of his own ego.

On retreat, we simply choose to remain with God. Mostly, there is silence in Adoration. Mostly, there is simply the will to remain in the presence of the One who revealed his love for us in Christ. That is our highest purpose in Adoration: I remain with God. As I keep choosing God, my habits of idolatry begin to fade, releasing their grip upon my heart and will. As I simply choose to remain with God, my need to be entertained, excited, distracted, and gratified becomes purified. The hold my idols have on my imagination wanes, and a new focus is born in my heart and mind. God is my all. This is not because Adoration carries any superficial immediate gratifications like my idols do. God does not pander to our cultural obsessions. No, Adoration is first the desert; over time it becomes the promised land fulfilling us with peace and communion, not frenzy and commotion. And it is the inner peace and communion with God that becomes our new desire. Such is the fruit of adoring the true God. We become simple and rest in what He shares. The deepest peace of communion is with him. No longer do we look for external satisfactions; we simply desire His presence as our rest and meaning.

The purpose of contemplative prayer is to gaze in love upon the mystery that is Christ revealed. To be a contemplative is to be drawn into the Life, Death, and Resurrection of Jesus as the foundational relationship of love in our life. As such, a contemplative deacon commits to entering regular communication with the living God simply because the deacon loves God. There are no expectations in this communication, no utilitarian motive to be with God; there is simply a desire to remain in God's presence.

As one enters this contemplative Adoration, engaging the mind and heart with the Scripture can assist one to remain with God. Praying with Scripture during Eucharistic Adoration is to be immersed in the vitality of faith; it is to be vulnerable to the peace and communion that God's presence brings to our interiority. What does a deacon "get out of" such prayer? Simply the fulfillment of his vocation as one called into discipleship with Christ. Being with Christ is prayer. Being with Christ is its own reward. Such vulnerability to Christ in the Eucharist and in the Scriptures invites the Holy Spirit to refashion us anew…to move us from "this passing age" (Rom. 12:1-2) into a life of communion with God. To live and minister as one in such communion situates one's effectiveness in evangelizing. Evangelizing occurs around a deacon who adores Christ and internalizes His Word within his own heart. Ministry is what happens around a deacon who prays. Ministry is not some separate goal or purpose. Ministry is not some skill set or competency. Serving people's spiritual and material needs and inviting their hearts to receive Christ's salvific love is what happens around a deacon who has become a contemplative.

Concretely, our time of Adoration might follow this pattern:

- Enter the chapel with only one expectation, "I will be in the Presence of God."
- Kneel or sit as you begin your prayer. First, surrender to Christ: "I am your deacon; I am yours; I am your follower…bless me. My diaconate is really your Diaconate — mediate your diaconal mission and mysteries through my heart for the sake of the people for whom you died; do with me what you will; speak to my heart; help me recognize your words."

- Dispose your heart to vulnerability. "Affect me however you want Christ. I trust you as the deepest love of my life. I open my heart so that our presences to one another can mature and become secure in my heart. I want our relationship to define my life."
- Spend some time in adoring and praising Christ as your Savior. Let gratitude arise. Slowly allow silence to rise in your heart and invite Christ to say whatever He wishes, or to say nothing. Delight in simply being alive through the love of God for a few minutes.
- When you wish, open the Scriptures and follow the *lectio divina* method shared above. This kind of prayer can make up a few minutes of your hour or a more significant portion. Simply follow any deepening sense of love, a growing faith, and a developing hope. As these virtues are longed for, then stay with *lectio divina*.
- After a while, return to silence. Just be in the Presence of God, asking for nothing, expecting nothing. Notice only what He wishes to gift you with in the form of a consoling emotion, a word of inspiration, a wordless peace,

an awareness of deepening communion, a blessing of your being, a fatherly healing, a needed purification, or simply the rest of silence.

- If it helps you remain in God's presence, write your prayer experience in your journal. The contents of this journal can be used for future spiritual direction sessions.
- At the end of the allotted time, you chose to pray, thank God and ask him to deepen your desire to choose to be with Him in this way. Give Him permission to call you into prayer all day long, to be your companion in life and not simply the object of a visit to Church.

Practical Matters

Adoration

"But one thing is necessary … "

— Luke 10:42

- If during this time you were completely distracted for the full hour, you are in very good company. Archbishop Fulton Sheen once remarked that in many of his daily 60-minute Adoration sessions it took him 57 minutes to struggle with what we're calling inner "*noise*"!
- So, be **patient** with yourself. God saw how you struggled. Remind yourself that God is present to you regardless of your ability to sense His Presence.
- Give thanks anyway; there is no such thing as wasting time before the Lord, broken earthen vessels that we are.

"Pray without ceasing. In all circumstances give thanks, for this is the will of God for you in Christ Jesus."

— 1 Thessalonians 5:17-18

What is Spiritual Direction on a Retreat?

The presence of a spiritual director on your retreat is a great gift of grace. He or she will generously listen to the content of your prayer as it intersects with your vocation and ministry. The primary aim of spiritual direction is to deepen your prayer life and as a result become more committed to prayer. Outside of this retreat, there is only one standard to judge the success of your time with a spiritual director: your prayer deepens, and you want to pray more. If that is the fruit of your spiritual direction, then you are with a good director.

During a retreat, the goals of spiritual direction are more modest and concentrated. The director on a retreat wishes to accompany you in conversation about what you are hearing God say in prayer. The director will assist you in listening to God, aid in your noticing God's movements in your heart, and point to places in your relationship with God that may need attention. By attention, we mean those areas of your life or your mode of communication with God that are not facilitating communion with Him.

It is helpful on this retreat — and in all sessions with a spiritual director — to not drift into therapy as one's specific focus. Our feelings will be relevant in spiritual direction, but attention to them in a therapeutic way is meant for another time and person.

In counseling, the person is directly talking through a life issue with a therapist. The dynamic of healing happens in this relationship with a counselor. In spiritual direction, one is being helped to notice and respond to the relationship that is happening between oneself and God. The spiritual director is a "third party," aiding the relationship between God and yourself. The director helps you learn to ask God to fulfill your desires, but first the director can help identify our real desires. God wants us to identify our desires so that He can purify them. Purification is done by your relating desires to the Paschal Mystery of Christ. We also invoke the Spirit, asking Him to raise our consciousness and recognize those desires of which we were previously unaware. So, in summary:

Spiritual direction assists a person to pay attention to:

- God coming toward us, in and through the affections (desires, thoughts, feelings).
- God inviting a deeper receptivity in us so as to host Him and notice any resistance to

intimacy with Him.
- God reaching out to us in experiences of transcendence, of times when we forget ourselves in beauty, truth, joy. Inside these experiences, God is moving.
- God purifying our egos by perhaps leaving our affections still or dry during prayer. But this experience of dryness needs to be discussed with the director because sometimes it indicates an area of resistance or desolation on our part.

Our desires lead us to God…our deepest desire is not for a thing or an event but for a relationship. Spiritual direction assists in clarifying what our deepest desires are and how to purify those which only direct us to superficial ends. With the help of media and technology, we stimulate these superficial desires, in the same way advertising works. Such superficial desires can direct us away from interiority, especially if maturing in the interior life promises a certain suffering in light of needed conversion. The director can help us to focus our desires and pray for the specific graces that internalize these desires. In such a dialogue with God, we see more clearly what we do want and what we do not want.

If we can discover what we want at the purest level of affect, rather than in passing moods or emotions disconnected from one's baptismal identity... then we can say that God wants those same ends. God is not making stuff up for me. God is moving me to choose Him out of my desire. In fulfilled desires are where His and your deepest intimacy exists. Following these desires in communion with Christ results in a vocation and further decisions that secure one's vocation. Your spiritual director will invite you to follow your desires in prayer. You may be invited to follow the pain (natural desolation, spiritual desolation, grief) and/or follow the peace (spiritual consolation from God, not simply a "good mood.') Peace or spiritual consolation always results in a deepening of faith, hope, and love.

Your spiritual director will help you say more to God about the peace or the pain. You do this by sharing your interior life with the Most Holy Trinity. As with all affections we:

- Acknowledge them
- Relate them to God (speak directly to the Trinity)

- Receive His love in return
- Respond to the Lord (pray again, seek forgiveness, give Him gratitude, change one's moral behavior, etc.)

What is Spiritual Consolation / Desolation?

Spiritual consolation is any affective movement that deepens our faith, hope, and love. They are enlivening emotions that carry within them the truth of God's love for us. They are His gift to us. We cannot "manufacture" them; we can only notice them and receive them. Once we receive, we are to internalize them through meditation and contemplation.

When you are in spiritual consolation, your spiritual director listens to you relate how you are staying with movements of the Holy Spirit. The director can affirm these movements theologically and invite you to deepen your prayer around these movements. He or she may also assist in identifying any resistance within you to fully receiving these consoling graces. If you are open, vulnerable, and able to relate your interior life to God, to receive His Love and presence, then the director stays out of the way. When this openness and communication are attained, the director just helps you say more about what God is giving you and how your intimacy with the Holy Trinity is deepening. The director helps you to stay in the presence of God receiving grace. The director reinforces your prayer experience with Scripture and assists your internalization of grace.

The spiritual director can also help us identify spiritual desolation. There is a natural desolation or sadness ("I lost a friend") or spiritual desolation ("I have resistance to the things of God"; "I have no desire to pray or worship"; "I have no desire for spiritual reading"; "I have lost interest in my ministry"; etc.). When spiritual desolation has been identified, we are called to reject it. Spiritual desolation is not "God's will" for you. Once identified, we are called to push against the desolation. We are, in other words, called to choose to engage our spiritual practices. If we do not want to pray, then our duty is to pray anyway. If we do not want to take up the Scriptures for *lectio divina*, we do so anyway, and so on. In doing this, soon God will move our desires to <u>want</u> intimacy with Him again.

In the case of natural desolation, we are called to relate such sadnesses to God. We are called to bring our losses and griefs to Him so that such sadness or depression can be addressed *within the relationship we have with God Himself* and not by myself, alone. God never wills that we bear natural desolations outside the communion He has with us in prayer, spiritual counsel, the sacraments, and fellowship with other believers.

Meditation Questions

Here are some questions your director may ask you: you can meditate upon them during your prayer and converse about them with the director.

What are your desires? Where do you sense the Spirit is moving you? What more can you say about the movements of desire? Can you notice where God is in these desires, affections, thoughts? Can you stay with God in these desires and thoughts and let Him communicate further with you?

Do you remember any time when you felt most intimate with God? In recalling this kind of prayer, can you return to it in your memory, alive in your heart, to receive more grace? Do you know that to receive God is a choice, it is active?

Do you know that when you receive God, your desires will change, and His consolations will come to define you?

> How did you pray? → What was its content? → What did you notice about your affective life? → What did God gift to you that increased your freedom? → Where were you struggling in prayer? → Was there anything in your prayer that made you resist his love or resist trusting him with more of yourself? →

Was there anyone you needed to forgive? → What new inspirations came from him for your ministry? → Was your prayer dry or empty of life?

Can you distinguish between your thoughts, feelings, and desires? Were you able to pray with your heart's desires? Were you led through your thoughts, feelings, and desires into the loving presence of the Holy Trinity? Did you pray with the saints or Blessed Virgin Mary? How did you experience the silence and solitude necessary for contemplative prayer? Are you able to integrate your personal prayer into liturgical worship? Are you able to notice your sinful temptations and bring them into prayer for healing? How will you allow prayer to come to you as you are ministering? Are you aware of the presence of Christ in your apostolic service?

Interior Silence

We had mentioned silence above, but there is more to this powerful virtue that should be emphasized. The goal on a retreat, and more profoundly when you leave retreat and return to ordinary life, is to cultivate interior silence. This silence, which comes to inhabit your soul as its normal condition, is the diminishment of interference between yourself and God. As your prayer matures, you will discover there is less "*noise*" that intrudes between yourself and God. A man of interior silence can turn very quickly from what preoccupies his mind due to duty or present interest to communion with God. God is no longer someone Whom you "work' to find; He inhabits you. The man of interior silence has learned how to refuse entry into his heart to any thought or feeling that undermines His communion with the Trinity. The trivia that used to concern him, the values of the "passing age" (1 Pet. 1:14; 1 Jn. 2:15; Rom. 12:1-2) have all been exposed to him as superficial. The interiorly silent man reserves his heart for communion with God. From this communion is born his thinking and acting. Such an interior life develops over time. It is a struggle to remain committed to relational prayer. With each time we enter prayer, however, we further the hope that the heart will become a place of interior silence. Such interior silence is a byproduct of prayer. We cannot will it. We cannot calculate its arrival. We focus upon God; we guard our thoughts; we choose virtue over sin; we become natives of the Eucharistic Liturgy and one day silence comes to replace the *"noise"* that currently defines the soul of the American male.

⌧

Conclusions

We invite you to offer any feedback you might think could improve our text, for the sake of future participants in IDR retreats.

idr@institutediaconalrenewal.org

Endorsements

"Silent retreats like the ones described by Deacon James Keating in this book have changed my life, and I can't imagine not doing an eight-day retreat every year. Deacons are required to take an annual retreat. In this short book, Deacons will find great help in entering into a silent retreat, which can at first seem daunting. What one always finds though is a deep encounter with the love of God. If silence is the language of God, then the human words in this small book will assist the heart hearing God speak. I commend the Institute for Diaconate Renewal for providing the diaconate with this invaluable resource for the renewal of the diaconate."

— The Most Rev. Andrew H. Cozzens
Bishop of Crookston, MN

"There are all sorts of reasons that people lapse into silence, but the theological reason for silence is 'affective maturity in the form of joy.' Silence results after contemplation meets truth, beauty, and goodness face-to-face. Keating masterfully explains first why we do silence, and second how to do silence. A superb and invaluable guide for the deacon."

— Dr. David Fagerberg
Professor Emeritus, University of Notre Dame

———

"In this short text, Deacon James Keating offers advice for entering into a retreat that is both substantial and practical. Whether a man is in formation, is newly ordained, or has been ordained for years, Deacon Keating's recommendations are sure to deepen the fruitfulness of a man's experience on retreat. Highly recommended."

— Chris Burgwald, STD
Chancellor of the Diocese of Sioux Falls

———

"I find this book to be both a practical and spiritual guide to a 'true' retreat. As one who prefers to 'do,' my first encounter with this format was personally challenging (to say it lightly), but the end results have strengthened my desire to diaconal ministry, and I now look forward to these times of contemplation. As usual, Deacon Keating has touched on the heart of the deacon and gives us practical application and reflection. My hope is that as Directors, we can ensure that all of the deacons under our care find a way to experience this Diaconal Retreat."

— Deacon Jim Grevenites
Director of Deacon Personnel,
Diocese of St. Petersburg
Chairman of the National Association
of Diaconate Directors (NADD)

About the Author

Dcn James Keating, PhD, is Professor of Spiritual Theology at Kenrick-Glennon Seminary in St Louis, MO. He was formerly Director of Deacon Formation for the Archdiocese of Omaha.

www.ingramcontent.com/pod-product-compliance
Lightning Source LLC
Chambersburg PA
CBHW070856050426
42453CB00012B/2235